A1+

I BET you CAN read!

The Joneses &
The Clan Trophy

Sous la direction de Michelle Jaillet
Frédéric André
Frédérique Denoix-Smart
Anne Doublet
Guillaume Ogier
Emmanuel Vesse

Illustrations de Mathieu Maillefer

MAGNARD

Meet the characters of your book!

The Joneses

They're twins and they have magic powers!

Amelia "Millie"

12 years old

She can freeze water and time. She controls lightning.

Oliver "Ollie"

12 years old

He can teleport.

Morph

Magic pet

He can transform into animals.

The McNights

They have magic powers too!

Octavia

13 years old

She can control animals and the weather.

Cadell

15 years old

He is the master of illusions.

Mink

Magic pet

She can transform into animals.

Chapter 1

It's the first day of the summer holidays. The Joneses are on holiday in Scotland. Amelia and Oliver are sitting outside in the garden.

Oliver: I love holidays! No homework and no tests, no getting up early... freedom at last!
Amelia: Yes, all this free time to read and relax... and to win this year's Clan Trophy!
Oliver: I know, I'm so excited!
Amelia: Me too!
Oliver: Hey, look! Morph is back! And he's got the invitation from the Clan Trophy Committee!
Amelia: Morph! Give me the invitation.

The Clan Trophy is a great challenge between two selected families with magic powers. They compete and the winner gets an incredible magic prize.

Oliver: What's the prize this year?

Amelia: Mind-reading glasses! With the glasses you know exactly what people think.

Oliver: That is so cool! Can you imagine? Getting the answers to Mrs Fletcher's terrible tests in advance!

Amelia: Ollie! The Trophy is a serious and very dangerous competition!

Oliver: Relax Millie, I know! And who are our competitors?

There is a purple and dark blue flash of light and suddenly two teenagers appear in front of the twins.

Oliver: Oh no! Not the McNights!

Chapter 2

Octavia: Well, well, well... Oliver and Amelia Jones, the most boring brother and sister on the planet!

Amelia: Octavia and Cadell McNight, the most arrogant brother and sister in the universe!

Cadell: In the universe? What a glorious introduction! Thank you!

Oliver: You are *not* welcome!

Octavia: How boring... We have no time for silly games, we are here to talk about the competition.
Cadell: And about our victory, of course.

Cadell and Octavia McNight come from a very powerful family. They have special powers like the Joneses'. They live in Scotland. They think they are royalty. They are rich, arrogant and they really hate the Joneses. Cadell and Octavia are determined to win.

Oliver: YOUR victory? You and your stupid fur animal have no chance of winning.
Octavia: Do you hear that, Mink?

Mink doesn't like the insult. She jumps from Octavia's neck onto the table showing her little pointed teeth and hissing at[1] *the Joneses. Next, Morph transforms into a fox to defend his master and mistress. Mink gets bigger and transforms into a lynx, ready to attack Morph. Morph jumps off the table and transforms into a wolf.*

1. *menacer en crachant (comme un chat)*

Cadell: What a show! Your pet can fight, but how about you?

Cadell extends his arms and a large cloud of dark blue night absorbs Oliver and Amelia. Suddenly the twins are not in Scotland anymore. They are in a dark forest. They are prisoners of a giant spider web. A monstrous hairy black spider with little red eyes is coming in their direction.

Oliver: Er, Millie, any idea?
Amelia: Ollie, remember! Cadell is the master of illusions. I know what to do.

A blue light appears around Amelia, she points her finger at the spider. BANG! There is a bright flash of light and the illusion disappears.

Cadell: Bravo! Bravo! Maybe you can fight after all.
Octavia: But you can't win. We have a... little surprise for you!

In a dark blue and purple flash of light, Cadell and Octavia suddenly disappear.

Chapter 3

It is Day 1 of the Clan Trophy competition. The McNights and the Joneses are with the Game Master in front of Loch Ness, in Scotland. There is an island in the middle of the lake.

Game Master: Welcome to the Clan Trophy competition! There are three different challenges and you must win two challenges to be the winning team.
The rules are simple: you mustn't kill anyone or anything, you can't teleport and you must be first to cross the finish line. Challenge n°1 is a race.
The first team to enter the castle on the island wins.
Good luck!
Oliver: Wow, Loch Ness in Scotland! Cool!
Amelia: And dangerous… there's Nessie the monster and other strange animals in the water…
Octavia: Are you scared? This is going to be so easy, come on Cadell!

Amelia: No worries, we just need to cross the lake to the island.

But the McNights make a quick start and jump first into one of the two small boats. Oliver and Amelia are right behind them. There are dark forms moving in the water in their direction.

Oliver: OMG! Millie, look, in the water! The Loch Ness monster!! And water snakes!
Amelia: Damn! It's Octavia. She can control animals and she is sending them.
Oliver: We only have two seconds to find a solution.
Amelia: I know. Octavia controls animals but I can freeze water. Ready to skate?

Amelia freezes the lake and imprisons the monsters in the ice. Quickly, Oliver and Amelia jump from their boat and skate on the frozen lake. Cadell and his sister are so surprised they can't react and they lose their first place. Oliver and Amelia get to the island and the water goes back to normal.

Oliver: That was great, Millie! I love skating!

Amelia: Let's go now!!!

Oliver and Amelia start running. The McNights are right behind them. Cadell extends his arms and creates a dense fog in front of the Joneses.

Oliver: Oh no! Can you see the door, Millie?

Amelia: No, I can't even see my hands!

Oliver: It's just one of Cadell's illusions. We need to find the entrance to the castle!

Oliver and Amelia continue running but they take the wrong direction. When the fog disappears, they can see Octavia and Cadell enter the castle. The McNights cross the finish line, they win the first challenge.

Cadell: Next time, remember I'm not just an illusionist, I'm the MASTER of illusions.

Octavia: Stupid Jones kids!

Amelia: This is not over! Next time we'll be ready.

Oliver: Yeah, time to get into warrior mode.

Chapter 4

It's Day 2 of the Clan Trophy competition. The Joneses, the McNights and the Game Master are in St James's Park, in London.

Game Master: Your second challenge is called "Find Morph and Mink". Morph and Mink are prisoners in a secret location in London. You must decipher an enigma, you must find your pets and rescue them.

The Game Master disappears.

Octavia: They what? They have Mink? And she's with that ridiculous Morph!
Oliver: Hey! Don't insult Morph! Your Mink...

Cadell looks at Octavia and they discreetly combine their powers. Octavia creates a strong wind and it takes Amelia's paper away. Then, Cadell creates the illusion of hundreds of little messages.

Amelia: Oh, no! Where's our enigma now? There are hundreds of them!

Octavia: Poor little Amelia! Come on Cadell, we need to rescue Mink.

They run away. Ten minutes later, Oliver and Amelia finally find the enigma and read it.

Morph and Mink are prisoners
but they can see the entire city.
Morph and Mink can touch the
sky but it's very cold and windy.
Three towers are old but their
tower is not.
Hurry, hurry, and find their
secret spot.

Amelia: We need to find a tower that is not old, well, it's not the Tower of London, and it's not the London Bridge towers... so... it must be the Shard!
Oliver: But of course! Millie, it's the Shard! It's new and it touches the sky! Let's go, quickly!

Oliver teleports them to the top of the Shard. When they arrive, the McNights are already there. The Joneses are on one side, the McNights are on the opposite side and the cage with Mink and Morph is just between them. Octavia starts using her powers but Amelia is ready to react.

Amelia: Oh no, you are not winning this challenge, no way!

Amelia raises her hands and she freezes time. The McNights stop moving and Amelia runs to the cage and liberates Mink and Morph. Then, time starts running again, and the Joneses are the winners this time.

Oliver: So you won one game and we won one game, it's a tie[1]. May the best team win!

Cadell looks at Octavia with a strange smile.

Cadell: Time for dirty tricks[2]...

1. *match nul* - 2. *C'est le moment de passer aux coups bas...*

Chapter 5

It's Day 3 of the Clan Trophy competition. The Joneses, the McNights and the Game Master are in front of a haunted castle in Scotland.

Game Master: This is your final challenge, and this one is particularly dangerous. A ghost lives in this castle: her name is the White Lady. Find her magic ring and bring it to me. Be careful, she doesn't like intruders. And one last thing: you mustn't use your powers for this challenge. Good luck!

Oliver, Amelia and Morph run into the cold, dark and creepy castle.

Amelia: Where is that ring? This castle is too big!
Oliver: Uh-oh...! The White Lady is behind you Millie! And... the ring is on her finger! Any idea how to take the ring?

Amelia: Ask her very politely?

Oliver: *(mocking)* "White Lady, sorry to intrude in your castle. Could you give us your magic ring, please?" It can't be that easy.

But the White Lady approaches silently and drops the ring into Oliver's hand.

Oliver: OK, so it was that easy!

Amelia: Er... Where are the McNights?

Oliver: Not our problem. We have the ring. Let's take it to the Game Master.

Oliver, Amelia and Morph run out of the castle and suddenly stop short. There's a gigantic red dragon with a black mark on its head in front of them, blocking their way.

Amelia: Is that Mink?

Oliver: No, it isn't. Look, Mink is behind the dragon with the McNights.

Cadell: Ah! You have the ring!

Octavia: Thanks for doing the job for us! Now give us the ring!

Oliver: What? No way!

Cadell: Well, your choice is this: you give us the ring or our family dragon, RedNight, turns you into barbecued Joneses!

Amelia: I don't believe it! They called a dragon! And they cheated[1].

---

1. *ils ont triché*

Octavia: Mink, can you go and get the ring, please?

Mink takes the ring from Oliver.

Octavia: Come on, Mink. Bring us the ring. Hurry up, RedNight is about to fire!
Cadell: Yeah, that crazy old dragon is so impulsive!

Mink hesitates. She looks at Morph for one second and then transforms into an eagle. She flies above RedNight and drops the ring into its big red mouth.

Cadell: Nooooo!! What did you do? The ring!
The flames! You destroyed it!

Chapter 6

RedNight the dragon doesn't look good. There is a sudden flash of light and the enormous dragon starts to get smaller and smaller and smaller! In a matter of seconds, the gigantic dragon is no more. The ring transformed RedNight into a cute little red dragonfly[1]!

1. *libellule*

Cadell: RedNight?! Is this a joke?

Octavia: I don't believe it, our family dragon… a dragonfly!?

Oliver: Come on Octavia, it's really cute!

Octavia: Wait until I turn your stupid cat into a fly!

The Game Master suddenly appears.

Game Master: Just calm down everybody! Ah, I see... Mink activated the ring's special protective power. She wanted to save Morph and the ring protected him from the dragon. And you can't reverse the magic, so... your family dragon is gone for ever.

Cadell: What?! We lost our ancestral family dragon because of Mink's stupid reaction?

Octavia: Mink!! Why did you do that?

Mink looks at Morph with love in the eyes, and Morph smiles back at her.

Amelia: Morph? What's wrong with you?

Oliver: Er… I think they're… in love, Millie.

Octavia: Mink, in love with your stupid cat?!

Amelia: Stop insulting our pet!

Oliver: They were prisoners together in that cage in London. They clearly became close friends.

The Game Master looks at Morph and Mink with a little smile. Then, he turns to the McNights. He looks very serious.

Game Master: Cadell and Octavia McNight, you cheated! So this year, the trophy goes to… Amelia and Oliver Jones! Congratulations to you, you are the winners of the Clan Trophy! Here is your prize.

The Game Master claps his hands and disappears. The mind-reading glasses magically appear in Amelia's hands. The McNights are gutted[1].

Octavia: What?! No! It can't be the end. I really need those mind-reading glasses.

Cadell: We were about to win and Mink, our pet, cost us the Clan Trophy!

Amelia: This is so cool! I can't wait to use them.

---

1. *dégoûtés, déçus*

Oliver: Yeah, and Mink and Morph are friends for life now. That's great too.

Cadell: Mink, come here now. Time to go home.

Mink hesitates but finally joins Octavia and Cadell. There is a purple and dark blue flash of light and suddenly the McNights are gone.

Epilogue

Amelia and Oliver are back in their holiday home, they are relaxing and drinking orange juice outside. Suddenly the McNights appear in a purple and dark blue flash of light.

Oliver: Can't you leave us alone?
Amelia: Ollie, wait. There's something wrong...

Cadell and Octavia look devastated.

Cadell: Something terrible happened! The Collector is back.

Amelia and Oliver look terrified when they hear that name.

Amelia: The Collector? You mean the evil wizard who kidnaps family pets to collect them and take their magic?
Octavia: Yes... and he has Mink!

Morph looks at Octavia. He looks in a panic.

Cadell: Morph is in danger too. We came to warn you and… to ask for your help.

Octavia: The Collector is so powerful and so dangerous. Cadell and I can't fight him alone.

Amelia puts the mind-reading glasses on. Everything Cadell says is true. Amelia, Oliver and Morph exchange looks, they make their decision. They don't really like the arrogant and nasty McNights but the danger is too great. It's time to unite their forces.

Oliver: Mink is a priority. We'll help and save her together!

Amelia: Collector, the Joneses and the McNights are coming for you!

Lexique

Chapter 1 (p. 5)

- **freedom:** *liberté*
- **at last:** *enfin*
- **mind-reading glasses:** *lunettes pour lire dans les pensées*
- **flash of light:** *éclair de lumière*
- **appear:** *apparaître*

Chapter 2 (p. 7)

- **boring:** *ennuyeux*
- **powerful:** *puissant*
- **fur animal:** *animal à fourrure*
- **neck:** *cou*
- **fox:** *renard*
- **master:** *maître*
- **mistress:** *maîtresse*
- **wolf:** *loup*
- **hairy:** *poilu*
- **bright:** *lumineux, brillant*

Chapter 3 (p. 11)

- **rules:** *règles du jeu*
- **behind:** *derrière*
- **dark:** *sombre*
- **OMG!:** *Oh my God!*
- **freeze:** *geler*
- **fog:** *brouillard*
- **warrior:** *guerrier*

Chapter 4 (p. 15)

- **decipher:** *déchiffrer*
- **rescue:** *sauver*
- **secret spot:** *un endroit secret*
- **already:** *déjà*
- **no way:** *hors de question*
- **raise:** *lever*

Chapter 5 (p. 19)

- **haunted:** *hanté*
- **bring:** *apporter*
- **creepy:** *qui fait très peur*
- **eagle:** *aigle*
- **ring:** *anneau*

Chapter 6 (p. 23)

- **fly** *(nom)*: *mouche*
- **become:** *devenir*

Epilogue (p. 27)

- **wizard:** *sorcier*
- **warn:** *prévenir*
- **nasty:** *méchant*

Activités de fin de chapitre

À la fin de chaque chapitre, fais l'activité proposée pour vérifier que tu as bien compris. Puis passe au chapitre suivant !

www.lienmini.fr/5682-ibycr-01

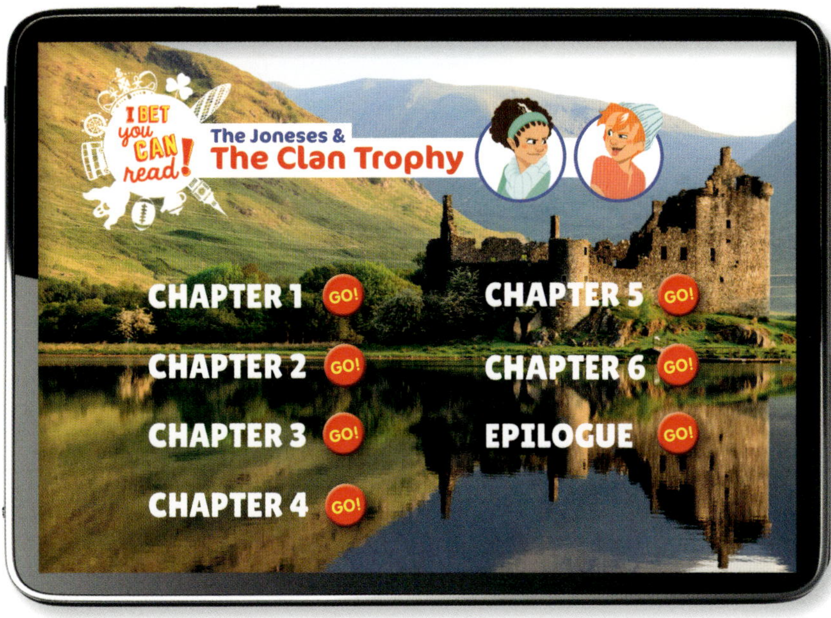

Did you like the story?
Tell the editor!

I Bet You Can Read!
Éditions Magnard
5, allée de la 2e D.B.
75015 Paris

Direction éditoriale et édition : Alexia Zoulas
Création graphique et mise en page : Cécile Chaumet
Illustrations, couverture et intérieur : Mathieu Maillefer
Relecture : Lee Smart
Enregistrements : EuroDVD
Responsable numérique : Dominique Garrigues

ISBN : 978-2-210-11568-2

5, allée de la 2e D.B.
75015 Paris
www.magnard.fr

PEFC 10-31-2065

Achevé d'imprimer en mars 2021 par Pollina en France - 97297
N° éditeur : MAGS120201073 - Dépôt légal : avril 2021